Family

One Hundred Quotes and Thoughts
With One Hundred Paintings of Lord Ganesha

R.N. Kogata • Lalita Kogata

D.K. Printworld (P) Ltd.
New Delhi

First published in India, 2012
ISBN 13: 978-81-246-0621-6
ISBN 10: 81-246-0621-8

A creation of:
Mr R N Kogata & Mrs Lalita Kogata
608, Hiran Magari, Sector-11, Udaipur - India
Phone : +91-94141-58870, +91-294-2583870
e-mail: devkush@rediffmail.com

Published and printed by:
D.K. Printworld (P) Ltd.
"Vedaśrī" F-395, Sudarshan Park
(Metro Station: Ramesh Nagar), New Delhi - 110 015
Phs.: 011-2545 3975, 2546 6019
Fax: 011-2546 5926
e-mail: indology@dkprintworld.com
Web: www.dkprintworld.com

Preface

Quotations are the fragrant spices of expression that season it to make it more palatable, more assimilative, more acceptable and more understandable. Even a single meaningful quotation can convey a message with much more efficacy that cannot be conveyed by a voluminous text.

This book contains 100 quotations on home, family and all one's near and dear within a family namely mother, father, son, daughter, brother, sister, baby, husband, wife, parents, grandparents and also on family relationships. Carefully chosen, mixed, modified or recreated, the quotes have been supported by the 100 paintings of the model family of Lord Shiva, comprising his consort Parvati and their children Ganesha and Kartik in the Hindu Pantheon, that will not only please you but will also expose you to an ideal family management. The paintings have been created by our team of professional artists keeping in mind the theme of each individual quote. The main objective of this book is to bring a family closer and make every individual understand the deep meaning of family bonding so as to change their attitudes towards fruitful and lasting relationships.

God has been very kind on us that we are living a very happy life ourselves but we have come across many people in distress or incidents within families, that have inspired us to produce this work on the family relations. We present this book with various quotes and thoughts, that should make the ties within families smoother, lovelier and stronger.

Some of the thoughts presented here are ours while others are from the people who have stood by and worked for the human values; some were famous names and some others were ordinary people. We have tried to indicate in the acknowledgement page, names of the persons whose quote we have reproduced, wherever we could remember. Any amendment/addition in this regard is most welcome from the learned readers.

Our sincere thanks to Agatha Christie, Barbara Alpert, Charles Wadsworth, Elbert Hubbard, Frederick W. Robertson, John Wooden Legs, Leonardo Di Caprio, Mildred B. Vermont, Oliver Wendell Holmes, Robert A. Heinlein, Sir Charles Gavan Duffy, Teresa Bloomingdale, Thomas Jefferson, Washington Irving and other eminent writers, who have given such invaluable thoughts to this world.

We prostrate before our parents Smt Kanchan Devi and Shri Bhairav Lal Kogata, and Smt Kamla Devi Nuwal and the late Prof K.M. Nuwal for their benign blessings that have guided us throughout and made us reach the stage where we find ourselves today.

With the expectation of blessings and constructive feedback from all of you.

Lalita and R.N. Kogata

Acknowledgements

Quotations of the following great personalities have been included in this book:

Page no.	By
7	Johann Wolfgang von Goethe
8	Christian Morgenstern
9	John Ed Pearce
10	Federick W. Roberston
11	Ellie Rodriguez
12	Mark Twain/ Frank A. Clark/ Carl Sandburg/ Charles Osgood/ Barretto/ Don Herrold
14	Eda J. Le Shan
15	Milwaukee Journal
16	Giri Graham Tchividjian
18	Washington Irving
19	Agatha Christie
20	Mildred B. Vermont
22	Renita Weems
23	Natasha Gregson Wagner
24	Meredith Gray
25	Milton Berle
26	Howard Johnson
27	Joseph Stefano/ Jewish proverb/ Victor Hugo/ Laurel Stephens/ Lisa Alther
28	T. DeWitt Talmage
29	Graycie Harmon
30	Margaret Culkin Banning
31	Oliver Wendell Holmes
36	Clarence Budington Kelland
37	Bartrand Hubbard
38	Harmon Killebrew
39	Ruth E. Renkel
40	Angelo Patri
43	Barbara Cage
44	Deanna Beisser
46	Joseph Addison
47	Epictetus
48	Charles Wadsworth
50	Walter M. Schirra, Sr.
52	Isadora James/ Marion C. Garretty/ Chris Montaigne/ Pam Brown

He is the happiest,
be he a king or a peasant,
who finds peace
in his home.

Home is —

- Not where you live but where they understand you the best.
- The place our feet may leave, but not our hearts.
- A shelter for storms — all sorts of storms!

Home

Home is a place,

you grow up in
but want to leave;

and when you grow old,
want to get back to.

Home is the one place in this entire world where hearts are sure of each other.

It is the place of strength and confidence.

It is the place where we tear off that mask of guarded and suspicious coldness that the world forces us to wear in self-defense, and where we pour out ourselves, communicate uninhibitedly with all the confiding hearts.

It is the place where expressions of tenderness gush out without any sensation of awkwardness, and without any dread of ridicule.

The light is what guides you home,

and the warmth is what keeps you there.

Baby

A baby —

- Has a special way of adding joy to every single day.
- Is an inestimable blessing and bother.
- Is born with a need to be loved and never outgrows it.
- Is God's sacred opinion that the world should go on.
- Is sunshine and moonbeams brightening your world as never before.
- Is a sweet new blossom of humanity on the earth.
- Is a link between angels and the mankind.
- Is always more joyful than you thought and more wonderful.
- Is bits of stardust blown from the hand of God.
- Is such a nice way to start a new generation.
- It touches the world with tender love.

A baby will make:
love stronger,
days shorter,
nights longer,
bankroll smaller,
home happier,
clothes shabbier,
the past forgotten,
and the future
worth living for.

A new baby is like
the beginning of all good things —

wonder, hope, dream,
and of
new possibilities.

A perfect example of
minority rule,

is a baby
in the house.

Children are not so different from kites…
children were created to fly.

But they need wind –
the under girding and strength
that comes from unconditional love,
encouragement, and prayer.

Mother

A man loves

his sweetheart the most;

his wife the best,

but his mother the longest.

Mother

Mother is the truest friend we have,

when trials heavy and sudden, fall upon us;

when adversity takes the place of prosperity;

when friends who rejoice with us
in our sunshine but desert us

when trouble thickens around us.

But the mother
still will cling to us,
and endeavour by her kind percepts
and counsel to dissipate
the clouds of darkness,
and thus cause peace
to return to our hearts.

A mother's love for her child,
is like nothing else in the world.

It knows no law, no pity;

it dares all things and crushes down
remorselessly all that stands in its path.

Being a full-time mother
is one of the highest paid jobs
in my field,
since the payment is
abundance of pure love.

God has bestowed every mother with –
fortitude, courage, tolerance, flexibility,
patience, firmness, sacrifice, blessings,
love, affection, faith, belief,
kindness, mercy and
nearly every other brave aspect
and kind virtue
of the great human soul.

I cannot forget my mother;
she is my bridge.

When I needed to get across,
she steadied herself
long enough for me
to run across safely.

I thought
my mom's whole and the only purpose
was to be my mom.

That's how she always made me feel.

I'd rather be a mother than anyone else on the earth
bringing up a child or two of unpretentious birth . . .

I'd rather tuck a little child all safe and sound in bed
than twine a chain of diamonds about my carefree head.

I'd rather wash a smudgy face with round, bright, baby eyes
than paint the pageantry of fame or walk among the wise.

If evolution really works,

how come mothers

only have two hands?

M is for the million things she gave me,
O means only that she's growing old,
T is for the tears she shed to save me,
H is for her heart of purest gold;
E is for her eyes, with love-light shining,
R means right, and right she'll always be,

Put them all together, they spell
"MOTHER,"

A word that means the world to me.

Mother –

- Is a child's best friend.
- Holds her children's hands for a while . . . their hearts forever.
- Understands what a child does not say.
- Arms are made of tenderness and children sleep soundly in them.
- Is there to support you, and hold you up whenever you need her.
- Could perform the jobs of several air traffic controllers with ease.

Mother — the bank
where we deposit
all our hurts and worries,
and yet it is always open.

Mother

My mom is a never ending song,
in my heart, comfort, happiness, and being.

I may sometimes forget the words,
but I always remember the tune.

She never quite leaves
her children at home,

even when she doesn't
take them along.

Youth fades, love droops,
the leaves of friendship fall;

But . . .

A mother's secret hope,
outlives them all.

A truly rich man is one,

whose children run into his arms

when his hands are empty.

F Far more inclined than most to grant the wings.
A Allowing us to reach enchanted lands.
T Thorough gentleman fulfiling all our demands and needs.
H Helping out with a young and restless heart.
E Eager to see us reaching all heights without any problem.
R Remembering our passions more than others.

Put them all together and it will spell FATHER

A WORD that means the FUTURE to us.

Father is someone
who listens, suggests
and defends.

A father can be one
of your very best friends!

Father Teaches Us —

Leadership: the personal reward of standing tall,
the challenge and excitement of taking any call.

Discipline: the self-awareness of staying with the show,
the calm respect of self-control.

Responsibility: the common sense of knowing when to care,
the moral obligation of providing and to share.

Generosity: the unselfishness of giving,
the peace of mind for forgiving.

Patience: the inner peace of not jumping the gun,
the gentle solitude of relaxing in the sun.

Courage: the satisfaction of doing
what is right,
and the pride and honour
to stand up and fight.

He didn't tell me how to live;

he lived,

and let me watch him do it.

I've had a hard life,
but my hardships are nothing
against the hardships,
that my father went through;
in order to get me
to where I am today.

My father used to play
with my brother
and me in the yard.

Mother would come out and say,

"You're tearing up the grass."
"We're not tearing the grass,"

Dad would reply:
"We're raising the boys."

Father

Sometimes

the poorest man

leaves for his children

the richest inheritance!

Father

The father
who would taste
the essence of his fatherhood,
must turn back from
the plane of his experience,
take with him
the fruits of his journey
and begin again beside his child,
marching step by step
over the same old road.

What makes a DAD

God took —

- The strength of a mountain,
- The majesty of a tree,
- The warmth of a summer sun,
- The calm of a quiet sea,
- The generous soul of nature,
- The comforting arm of night,
- The wisdom of the ages,
- The power of the eagle's flight,
- The joy of a morning in spring,
- The faith of a mustard seed,
- The patience of eternity,
- The depth of a family need,
- Then God combined these qualities,
- When there was nothing more to add,
- He knew His masterpiece was complete,

And so,

He called it ... Dad.

Daughter

A daughter is —

- A day brightener and a heart warmer.
- A God's gift of love.
- A little girl who grows up to be a great friend.
- A mother's gender partner, her closest ally in the family confederacy, an extension of her self.
- A treasure and a cause of sleeplessness.
- One of the most beautiful gifts this world has to give.
- May outgrow your lap, but she will never outgrow your heart.

A daughter
is a bundle of firsts
that excite and delight,
giggles that come from deep inside
and are always contagious;
everything wonderful and precious
and your love for her knows no bounds.

A daughter is a miracle
that never ceases to be miraculous . . .
full of beauty and forever beautiful . . .
loving, caring and truly amazing.

A daughter is:

the happy memories of the past,
the joyful moments of the present,
and the hope and promise of the future!

Daughter

Certain is that
there is no kind of affection,
so purely angelic as of a father
to a daughter.

In love to our wives there is desire;
to our sons, ambition;
but to our daughters
there is something for which,
there are no words to express.

Son

Be careful to leave your sons
well instructed rather than rich;
for the hopes of the instructed
are better than the wealth of the ignorant.

By the time a man realises
that may be his father was right,

he usually has a son
who thinks he's wrong!

Giving your son a good skill,

is better than giving him

one thousand pieces of gold.

Son

You don't raise heroes,
you raise sons.

And if you treat them like sons,
they'll turn out to be heroes,
even if it's just in your own eyes.

Son

Your son at five is your master,
at ten your slave,
at fifteen your double;

and after that, your friend
or your foe,
depending on his bringing up.

A sister —

- Is a gift to the heart, a friend to the spirit, a golden thread to the meaning of life.
- Is a little bit of childhood that can never be lost.
- Shares childhood memories and grown-up dreams.
- Smiles when one tells one's stories — for she knows where the decoration has been added.
- Is a friend who listens with her heart.

Sister

Having a sister is like
having a best friend,
you can't get rid of.

You know whatever you do,
they'll still be there.

Sister

She is your mirror,
shining back at you
with a world of possibilities.

She is your witness,
who sees you at your worst and best,
and loves you anyway.

She is your partner in crime,
your midnight companion,
someone who knows
when you are smiling, even in the dark.

She is your teacher,
your defense attorney,
your personal press agent,
even your shrink.

Someday, she's the reason when
you wish you were an only child.

Sisters probably are
the most competitive relationship
within the family;

but once the sisters are grown up,
it becomes the strongest relationship,
within the family.

Sister

The mildest, drowsiest sister
has been known to turn a tigress
if her sibling is in any trouble.

Brother

Brothers don't necessarily
have to say anything to each other —

they can sit in a room and be together
and just be completely comfortable
with each other.

Help your brother's boat across,

and your own will reach the shore!

Brother

It was nice growing up
with someone like you my brother —

someone to lean on,

someone to count on . . .

someone to tell on!

Brother

My brother my most beloved friend
and my bitterest rival,
my confidant and my betrayer,
my sustainer and my dependent,
and scariest of all, my equal!

Brother

To the outside world we all grow old,
but not to our brothers and sisters.

We know each other as we always were,
we know each other's hearts.

We share private family jokes,
we remember family feuds, secrets, sorrows and joys;
we live outside the touch of time.

A caring husband
hears the song in his wife's heart,
and sings it to the wife
when her memory fails.

A husband is the dream and the destination,
ultimate truth and unlimited shine,
pride and honour
and a true friend and companion
for the caring wife.

Husband

Just as a good tree
with scented flowers,

makes the entire forest
perfumed and pleasant;

so does a good husband
enhance the confidence, love
and happiness of his wife.

The nature of all men
is always the same;

it is their habits
which make them a perfect husband.

Husband

What is a husband?

He is the one who, with a touch,
can bring back the starlight
and glow of the years long gone by.

At least he hopes he can —
don't disappoint him.

Never discourage him.

A faithful and loving wife

is the jewel of a successful marriage!

A man's wife has
more power over him
than the state has!

A caring wife

is the joy

of a man's heart.

My best chosen friend,
companion and guide,
to walk through life,
linked hand-in-hand;

two equal, loving friends,
true husband and true wife.

Wife

Only two things are necessary
to keep one's wife happy.

One is to let her think
she is having her own way,
and the other is
to let her have it.

A parent
who has never apologised
to his children,
is a monster.

If he's always apologising,
his children are monsters.

Don't handicap your children

by making their lives easy.

Don't worry that children never listen to you;

worry that they are always watching you.

Each day of our lives
we make deposits,
in the memory banks
of our children!

Parents

If I had my child to raise all over again:

I'd build self-esteem first, and the house later.

I'd finger-paint more, and point the finger less.

I would do less correcting and more connecting.

I'd take my eyes off my watch, and watch with my eyes.

I'd take more hikes and fly more kites.

I'd stop playing serious, and seriously play.

I would run through more fields and gaze at more stars.

I'd do more hugging and less tugging.

Parents

Parents are the wonderful people who give just so much,
and who bring joy to the lives that they touch.

Parents are the two special people who are willing to share,
and who are never too busy to listen and care.

Parents are the ones who encourage and patiently guide,
and who think of their children with enormous pride.

And because their devotion and loving is true,
their family ties last a whole lifetime through.

There are two lasting bequests
we can give our children:

One is roots.
The other is wings.

Your children need your presence,

more than your presents.

A grandfather is someone

with silver in his hair

and gold in his ear.

A grandmother is
little bit a parent,
little bit a teacher, and
little bit a best friend.

Everyone needs to have access,
both to grandparents and grandchildren,
in order to be a full human being.

Grandchildren are
God's way of compensating us
for growing old.

Grandma —

- Serves kisses and counsel daily.
- Are moms with lots of frosting.
- Heart is a patchwork of Love.
- Hold our tiny hands for just a little while, but our hearts forever.
- Never run out of hugs or cookies.
- A wonderful mother with lots of practice.
- Are just "antique" little girls.
- Is a mother who has a second chance.
- Is a safe haven.
- Is a special person who causes a joyful happening in the heart of a child.

Grand Parents

Grandparents are
a delightful blend of laughter,
caring deeds,
wonderful stories
and lots of Love . . .

If I had known
how wonderful it would be
to have grandchildren,
I'd have had them first!

If your baby is

"beautiful and perfect,
never cries or fusses,
sleeps on schedule
and burps on demand,
an angel all the time,"

you're the "Grandma"!

Our grandchildren accept us
for ourselves, without rebuke
or effort to change us,

as no one in our entire lives
has ever done,

not our parents, siblings,
spouses, friends —

and hardly ever our
own grown up children.

Our land is everything to us. . . .

I will tell you one of the things
we remember on our land.

We remember our grandfathers paid for it —
with their life.

To become a grandparent
is to enjoy one of the few pleasures
in life,
for which the consequences
have already been paid.

What children need most
are the essentials,
that grandparents provide
in abundance.

They give unconditional love,
kindness, patience, humor, comfort,
and unfailing lessons in life.

And, most importantly, cookies.

Families are the compass that guides us.

They are the inspiration to reach great heights,
and our comfort
when we occasionally falter.

Family faces are the magic mirrors.

Looking at the people
who belong to us,
we see
the past, present, and future.

Feelings of worth can flourish only in an atmosphere where individual differences are appreciated, mistakes are tolerated, communication is open, and rules are flexible —

the kind of atmosphere
that is found in a nurturing family.

If minutes were kept of a family gathering,
they would show that "Members not Present"
and "Subjects Discussed"
were one and the same!

In dwelling, live close to the ground.
In thinking, keep to the simple.
In conflict, be fair and generous.
In governing, don't try to control.
In work, do what you enjoy.
In family life, be completely present.

No matter what you've done
for yourself or for humanity,
if you can't look back
on having given love and attention
to your own family,
what have you really accomplished?

One of the best parts of being a family is that you can encourage one another.

You can believe in one another.

You can affirm one another.

The family you come from,
isn't as important as the
family you're going to have!

The happiest moments of my life
have been the few,
which I have passed at home
in the bosom of my family.

To us, family means
putting your arms around each other
and being there.

Don't smother each other;

no one can grow in the shade.

Lust is easy.

Love is hard.

Like is most important.

Relationship

Smile at each other,
smile at your wife,
smile at your husband,
smile at your children,
smile at each other —

it doesn't matter who it is —

and that will help you
to grow up in greater love
for each other.

To know when to go away
and when to come closer,
is the key
to any lasting relationship.

You can kiss your family and friends
good-bye and put miles between you,
but at the same time
you carry them with you
in your heart, your mind, your stomach,
because you do not just live in a world
but a world lives in you.